An index to Captain Armstrong's map of Lincolnshire: shewing the names and number of the grand divisions and wapon-takes, with the parishes, in alphabetical order

Andrew Armstrong

An index to Captain Armstrong's map of Lincolnshire: shewing the names and number of the grand divisions and wapon-takes, with the parishes, in alphabetical order. ... N.B. an index to be given (gratis) to subscribers with each map, which will be published in January 1779.

Armstrong, Andrew
ESTCID: T203241
Reproduction from Bodleian Library (Oxford)
The Map of Lincolnshire was published in 1778-9.
[Lincoln?, 1778].
39,[1]p. ; 8°

Eighteenth Century
Collections Online
Print Editions

Gale ECCO Print Editions

Relive history with *Eighteenth Century Collections Online*, now available in print for the independent historian and collector. This series includes the most significant English-language and foreign-language works printed in Great Britain during the eighteenth century, and is organized in seven different subject areas including literature and language; medicine, science, and technology; and religion and philosophy. The collection also includes thousands of important works from the Americas.

The eighteenth century has been called "The Age of Enlightenment." It was a period of rapid advance in print culture and publishing, in world exploration, and in the rapid growth of science and technology – all of which had a profound impact on the political and cultural landscape. At the end of the century the American Revolution, French Revolution and Industrial Revolution, perhaps three of the most significant events in modern history, set in motion developments that eventually dominated world political, economic, and social life.

In a groundbreaking effort, Gale initiated a revolution of its own: digitization of epic proportions to preserve these invaluable works in the largest online archive of its kind. Contributions from major world libraries constitute over 175,000 original printed works. Scanned images of the actual pages, rather than transcriptions, recreate the works *as they first appeared.*

Now for the first time, these high-quality digital scans of original works are available via print-on-demand, making them readily accessible to libraries, students, independent scholars, and readers of all ages.

For our initial release we have created seven robust collections to form one the world's most comprehensive catalogs of 18th century works.

Initial Gale ECCO Print Editions collections include:

History and Geography

Rich in titles on English life and social history, this collection spans the world as it was known to eighteenth-century historians and explorers. Titles include a wealth of travel accounts and diaries, histories of nations from throughout the world, and maps and charts of a world that was still being discovered. Students of the War of American Independence will find fascinating accounts from the British side of conflict.

Social Science
Delve into what it was like to live during the eighteenth century by reading the first-hand accounts of everyday people, including city dwellers and farmers, businessmen and bankers, artisans and merchants, artists and their patrons, politicians and their constituents. Original texts make the American, French, and Industrial revolutions vividly contemporary.

Medicine, Science and Technology
Medical theory and practice of the 1700s developed rapidly, as is evidenced by the extensive collection, which includes descriptions of diseases, their conditions, and treatments. Books on science and technology, agriculture, military technology, natural philosophy, even cookbooks, are all contained here.

Literature and Language
Western literary study flows out of eighteenth-century works by Alexander Pope, Daniel Defoe, Henry Fielding, Frances Burney, Denis Diderot, Johann Gottfried Herder, Johann Wolfgang von Goethe, and others. Experience the birth of the modern novel, or compare the development of language using dictionaries and grammar discourses.

Religion and Philosophy
The Age of Enlightenment profoundly enriched religious and philosophical understanding and continues to influence present-day thinking. Works collected here include masterpieces by David Hume, Immanuel Kant, and Jean-Jacques Rousseau, as well as religious sermons and moral debates on the issues of the day, such as the slave trade. The Age of Reason saw conflict between Protestantism and Catholicism transformed into one between faith and logic -- a debate that continues in the twenty-first century.

Law and Reference
This collection reveals the history of English common law and Empire law in a vastly changing world of British expansion. Dominating the legal field is the *Commentaries of the Law of England* by Sir William Blackstone, which first appeared in 1765. Reference works such as almanacs and catalogues continue to educate us by revealing the day-to-day workings of society.

Fine Arts
The eighteenth-century fascination with Greek and Roman antiquity followed the systematic excavation of the ruins at Pompeii and Herculaneum in southern Italy; and after 1750 a neoclassical style dominated all artistic fields. The titles here trace developments in mostly English-language works on painting, sculpture, architecture, music, theater, and other disciplines. Instructional works on musical instruments, catalogs of art objects, comic operas, and more are also included.

The BiblioLife Network

This project was made possible in part by the BiblioLife Network (BLN), a project aimed at addressing some of the huge challenges facing book preservationists around the world. The BLN includes libraries, library networks, archives, subject matter experts, online communities and library service providers. We believe every book ever published should be available as a high-quality print reproduction; printed on-demand anywhere in the world. This insures the ongoing accessibility of the content and helps generate sustainable revenue for the libraries and organizations that work to preserve these important materials.

The following book is in the "public domain" and represents an authentic reproduction of the text as printed by the original publisher. While we have attempted to accurately maintain the integrity of the original work, there are sometimes problems with the original work or the micro-film from which the books were digitized. This can result in minor errors in reproduction. Possible imperfections include missing and blurred pages, poor pictures, markings and other reproduction issues beyond our control. Because this work is culturally important, we have made it available as part of our commitment to protecting, preserving, and promoting the world's literature.

GUIDE TO FOLD-OUTS MAPS and OVERSIZED IMAGES

The book you are reading was digitized from microfilm captured over the past thirty to forty years. Years after the creation of the original microfilm, the book was converted to digital files and made available in an online database.

In an online database, page images do not need to conform to the size restrictions found in a printed book. When converting these images back into a printed bound book, the page sizes are standardized in ways that maintain the detail of the original. For large images, such as fold-out maps, the original page image is split into two or more pages

Guidelines used to determine how to split the page image follows:

• Some images are split vertically; large images require vertical and horizontal splits.
• For horizontal splits, the content is split left to right.
• For vertical splits, the content is split from top to bottom.
• For both vertical and horizontal splits, the image is processed from top left to bottom right.

An I N D E X

To Captain ARMSTRONG's

MAP of LINCOLNSHIRE:

S H E W I N G

The Names and Number of the Grand Divifions and Wapon-
takes, with the Parifhes, in alphabetical Order.

The whole digefted into proper Columns, with Letters of
Reference on the Margin of the Map, for the ready finding
of any Place, by Infpection.

Alfo a Scheme of the Turnpike and other Roads, with the
Diftance of Miles on each, from LINCOLN MINSTER.

To which are added Tables of the Tides, and Time of paffing
over *Crofs-Key* and *Fofdike* Wafhes.

And alfo the Time of paffing the Ferry, between *Barton* and *Hull*.

N. B. An Index to be given (gratis) to Subfcribers with each Map,
which will be publifhed in January 1779.

LINCOLNSHIRE is in three Grand Divisions, viz. LINDSEY, KESTEVEN, and HOLLAND; and each of them is divided into *Hundreds*, or *Wapontakes*, and these again into *Parishes*; Lindsey by far the largest Division has seventeen *Wapontakes*, Kesteven ten, and Holland three; in all thirty, in which are 630 Parishes, besides a number of Chapels, and religious Houses, not in use; also a number of Places that are extra-parochial, as belonging to no Parish; and some few Parishes that claim an Exemption from ecclesiastical Jurisdiction; as *Revcesby, Tattershall, Little Grimsby,* &c.

LINDSEY.

Aslacoe,	Asla.
Bollingbrooke,	Bol.
Bradly,	Brad.
Calceworth,	Cal.
Candleshoe,	Cand.
Corringham,	Cor.
Gartree,	Gar.
Hill,	Hill
Horncastle,	Horn.
Lawres,	Law.
Louth Eske,	Lou.
Ludborough	Lud.
Manley,	Man.
Welshcroft,	Wel.
Well,	Well.
Wraggoe	Wrag.
Yarborough,	Yarb.

KESTEVEN.

Aveland,	Ave.
Aswardburn,	Asw.
Beltisloe,	Bell.
Boothby Graffoe,	Boo.
Flaxwell,	Flax.
Grantham,	Gran.
Langoe,	Lang.
Lovedon,	Lov.
Ness,	Ness.
Winnibriggs,	Winn.

HOLLAND

Elloe,	Ell.
Kirton	Kirt.
Skirbeck,	Skir.

THE

THE following Scheme of this Index is divided into Columns; in the firft are the Names of Parifhes, in alphabetical Order, in the fecond is the Name, or Abbreviation, of the Wapontake; in the third, the Name of the grand Divifion; and in the laft Column are two large Letters, anfwering to thofe engraved on the Scale, or Margin of the Map, with Lines drawn perpendicular and horizontal, which divides the whole Map into Squares: And obferve where the Lines from thefe two Letters meet, or near it, you will find the Situation of the Place wanted: But an Example will make all plain.

Suppofe you want to find Barton on the Map. Look in the firft Column for Barton, againft it is Yarborough, next is Lindfay, and oppofite, in the laft Column, is A and D.

Which, with a little Practice will become familiar and eafy; but without fuch a Scheme, it would be tedious to find out any Place wanted, on fo large a Map.

NAME

NAME and NUMBER
OF
PARISHES,
IN
ALPHABETICAL ORDER.

Names.	Wapontakes.	Grand Division.	Letters.
A			
Aby,	Cal.	Lindsey,	G. G.
Addlethorpe,	Can.	Lindsey,	G. H.
Ailsby,	Brad.	Lindsey,	C. E.
Aisthorpe	Lawr.	Lindsey,	F. C.
Algarchurch,	Kirb.	Holland,	L. F.
Altord,	Cal.	Lindsey,	G. G.
Alkborough,	Yar.	Lindley,	B. B.
Allington, east,	Winn.	Kesteven,	L. B.
Allington, west,	Winn.	Kesteven,	L. B.
Althorpe,	Man.	Lindsey,	C. B.
Althorpe, near Louth,	Lou.	Lindsey,	G. G.
Alvinghame,	Low.	Lindsey,	F. G.
Ancaster,	Lov.	Kesteven,	K. C.
Anderby,	Cal.	Lindsey,	G. H.
Anwick,	Flax.	Kesteven,	K. D.
Appleby,	Man.	Lindsey,	B. C.
Apply,	Wrag.	Lindsey,	G D.
Asgarby,	Asw.	Kesteven,	r. D.
Asgarby, near Horncastle,	Bol.	Lindsey,	H. F.
Ashby de la Land,	Horn.	Lindsey,	G. F.
Ashby Chapel,	Flax.	Kesteven,	I. D.
Ashby by Spilsby,	Cand.	Lindsey,	H. G.
Ashby Puerorum,	Hill.	Lindsey,	H. F.
Ashby, near Grimsley,	Brad.	Lindsey,	D. F.

Names.	Wapontakes.	Grand Division.	Letters.
Aſlackby,	Ave.	Kefteven,	M. D.
Aſterby,	Gar.	Lindſey,	G. F.
Aiwardby,	Hill.	Lindſey,	H. G.
Aſwardby,	Aſw.	Kefteven,	L. D.
Aubourn,	Boo.	Kefteven,	H. B.
Aunſby,	Aſw.	Kefteven,	L. D.
Authorpe,	Louth.	Lindſey,	G. G.
B.			
Bamburgh,	Gar.	Lindſey,	G. E.
Barkwith, eaſt,	Wrag.	Lindſey,	F. E.
Barkwith, weſt,	Wrag.	Lindſey,	F. E.
Barton, St. Mary,	Yar.	Lindſey,	A. D.
BARTON, St. Peter,	Yar.	Lindſey,	A. D.
Barkſton,	Gran.	Kefteven,	K. C.
Barlow,	Yar.	Lindſey,	A. D.
Barnetby le world,	Yar.	Lindſey,	C. D.
Barnetby le beck,	Brad.	Lindſey,	D. E.
Bardrey,	Wrag.	Lindſey,	H. D.
Barrowby,	Winn.	Kefteven,	L. B.
Barholm,	Neſs.	Kefteven,	O. D.
Barling,	Lawr.	Lindſey,	G. D.
Faſtinghame,	Boo.	Kefteven,	H. B.
Baſſingthorpe,	Bell.	Kefteven,	M. C.
Baſton,	Neſs.	Kefteven,	O. D.
Beckinghame,	Lov.	Kefteven,	I. B.
Beeſby,	Brad.	Lindſey,	D F.
Beelby,	Cal.	Lindſey,	G. G.
Belton,	Man.	Lindſey,	C. A
Belton,	Gren.	Kefteven,	L C.
Belchford,	Gar.	Lindſey,	G. F.
Belleau,	Cal.	Lindſey,	G. G.
Bernyworth,	Wrag.	Lindſey,	F. E.
Bennington, long,	Love.	Kefteven,	I. B.
Bennington,	Skir	Holland,	K G.
Bicker,	Kirt.	Holland,	L. E.

Bigby,

Names.	Wapontakes.	Grand Division.	Letters.
Bigby,	Yar.	Lindfey,	C. D.
Billby,	Cal.	Lindfey,	G. H.
Billinghay,	Lang.	Kefteven,	I. B.
Billingborough,	Ave.	Kefteven,	L. D.
Binbrook, St. Mary,	Wal.	Lindfey,	E. E.
Binbrook, St. Gabriel,	Wal.	Lindfey,	E. E.
Bifkerthorpe,	Gar.	Lindfey,	F. E.
Bitchfield,	Bell.	Kefteven,	M. C.
Blankney,	Lang.	Kefteven,	I. D.
Bloxholm,	Flax.	Kefteven,	I. D.
Blyburgh,	Alas.	Lindfey,	E. C.
Blyton,	Cor.	Lindfey,	E. B.
Boatham,	Boo.	Kefteven,	H. C.
Bottesford,	Man.	Lindfey,	C. B.
BOLLINGBROKE,	Bol.	Lindfey,	H. G.
Bonby,	Yar.	Lindfey,	B. C.
Boothby, Pagnel,	Winn.	Kefteven,	M. C.
Boothby,	Boo.	Kefteven,	I. C.
BOSTON,	Skir.	Holland,	K. F.
BOURN,	Ave.	Kefteven,	M. D.
Brattleby,	Afla.	Lindfey,	F. C.
Branflon,	Lincoln Liberty	Kefteven,	H. B.
Bracebridge,	Liberty of Linc.	Kefteven,	H. C.
Braceby,	Gran.	Kefteven,	L. C.
Brant, Broughton,	Love.	Kefteven,	I. B.
Braceborough,	Nefs.	Kefteven,	O. D.
Brancewell,	Flax.	Kefteven,	I. D.
Bratoft,	Cand.	Lindfey,	H. H.
Bradley,	Brad.	Lindfey,	E. E.
Frifkhill,	Hill.	Lindfey,	G. G.
Brigfley,	Brad.	Lindfey,	D. F.
Broughton,	Man.	Lindfey,	C. C.
Broxholm,	Lawr.	Lindfey,	F B.
Brough in the Marfh,	Cand.	Lindfey,	H. H.
Brothertoft,	Kirt.	Holland,	K. F.
Brocklefby,	Yar.	Lindfey,	C. E.

Bucknall,

Names.	Wapontakes.	Grand Division.	Letters.
Bucknall,	Gar.	Lindfey,	H. E.
Burton Strather,	Man.	Lindfey,	B. B.
Burton by Lincoln,	Lawr.	Lindfey,	G. C.
Burton, Cogles,	Bell.	Kefteven,	M. C.
Burton, Pedwardine,	Afw.	Kefteven,	L. D.
Burgh on Bain,	Wrag.	Lindfey,	I. E.
Burwell,	Lou.	Lindfey,	G. G.
Bullingthorpe,	Law.	Lindfey,	F. D.
Butterwick, weft,	Man.	Lindfey,	C. B.
Butterwick, eaft,	Skir.	Holland,	K. G.
Bytham parva,	Bell.	Kefteven,	N. C.
Bytham Caftle,	Bell.	Kefteven,	N. C.
C.			
Cabourn,	Brad.	Lindfey,	D. E.
Cadney,	Yar.	Lindfey,	D. C.
Cainby,	Alas.	Lindfey,	C. C.
CAISTORTHONG,	Yar.	Lindfey,	D. E.
Calceby,	Cal.	Lindfey,	G. G.
Calkwell,	Gar.	Lindfey,	G. F.
Calverthorpe,	Afw.	Kefteven,	L. D.
Calfthorpe,	Lou.	Lindfey,	G. G.
Cameringhame,	Alas.	Lindfey,	F C.
Canwick,	Lincoln Liberty	Kefteven,	H. C.
Candlefby,	Cand.	Lindfey,	H. G.
Careby,	Bell.	Kefteven,	N. C.
Carleby,	Nefs.	Kefteven,	N. D.
Carlton, Moorland,	Boo.	Kefteven,	I. B.
Carlton fcroop,	Lov.	Kefteven,	K. C.
Carlton magna,	Lou.	Lindfey,	F. G.
Carlton parva,	Lou.	Lindfey,	F. G.
Carlton Caftle,	Lou.	Lindfey,	F. G.
Carlton, north,	Lawr.	Lindfey,	F. C.
Carlton, fouth,	Lawr.	Lindfey,	G. C.
Cawthorpe,	Cal.	Lindfey,	G. G.
Caythorpe,	Lov.	Kefteven,	K. C.

Claxby,

Names.	Wapontakes.	Grand Division.	Letters.
Claxby,	Wal.	Lindfey,	E. D.
Claxby, near Well,	Cal.	Lindfey,	G. G.
Claxby, pluckacre,	Hill.	Lindfey,	H. F.
Claypoole,	Love.	Kefteven,	K. B.
Clee,	Brad.	Lindfey,	C. F.
Clixby,	Yar.	Lindfey,	D. D.
Coats in the Moor,	Afla.	Lindfey,	F. B.
Coats, north,	Brad.	Lindfey,	E. H.
Coats, magna,	Brad.	Lindfey,	C. E.
Coats, parva,	Brad.	Lindfey,	C. F.
Cockerington, magna,	Lou.	Lindfey,	F. G.
Cockerington, St. Leonard,	Lou.	Lindfey,	F. G.
Coleby,	Boo.	Kefteven,	H. C.
Colterfworth,	Gran.	Kefteven,	M. C.
Coningfby,	Horn.	Lindfey,	I. E.
Coningsholme,	Lou.	Lindfey,	E. G.
CORBY,	Bell.	Kefteven,	M. C.
Covenham, St. Bartholomew,	Lud.	Lindfey,	E. G.
Covenham, St. Mary,	Lud.	Lindfey,	E. G.
Cowbit,	Ell.	Holland,	N. F.
Cranwell,	Flax.	Kefteven,	K. C.
Creeton,	Bell.	Kefteven,	N. C.
Croft,	Cand.	Lindfey,	I. H.
Crowle,	Man.	Lindfey,	B. A.
Crowland,	Ell.	Holland,	N. F.
Croxby,	Wal.	Lindfey,	D. E.
Croxton,	Yar.	Lindfey,	C. D.
Cumberworth,	Cal.	Lindfey,	G. H.
Cuxwold,	Brad.	Lindfey,	D. E.

D.

Dalby,	Cand.	Lindfey,	G. G.
Dalderby,	Gar.	Lindfey,	H. F.
DEEPING MARKET,	Nefs.	Kefteven,	O. E.
Deeping, St. James,	Nefs.	Kefteven,	O. E.
Deeping, weft,	Nefs.	Kefteven,	O. D.

B

Dembleby,

Names.	Wapontakes.	Grand Division.	Letters.
Dembleby,	Ave.	Kesteven,	L. D.
Denton,	Gran.	Kesteven,	L. B.
Digby,	Flax.	Kesteven,	I. D.
Durington,	Flax.	Kesteven,	I. D.
Doddington, north,	Boo.	Kesteven,	H. B.
Doddington, south,]	Lov.	Kesteven,	K. B.
Donington,	Kirt.	Holland,	L. C.
Donington on Bain,	Gar.	Lindsey,	F. F.
Dousby,	Ave.	Kesteven,	M. E.
Driby,	Cand.	Lindsey,	G. G,
Duniton,	Lang.	Kesteven,	H. D.
Dunsby,	Ave.	Kesteven,	M. D.
Dunholm,	Lawr.	Lindsey,	F. C.
E.			
Eagle,	Boo.	Kesteven,	H. B.
Edenham, with Grimthorpe,	Bell.	Kesteven,	N. D.
Edlington,	Gar.	Lindsey,	G. E.
Elkington, north,	Lou.	Lindsey,	E. F.
Elkington, south,	Lou.	Lindsey,	F. F.
Elsham,	Yar.	Lindsey,	C. D,
Enderby Bag,	Hill.	Lindsey,	G. F.
Enderby Wood,	Horn.	Lindsey,	H. F.
Enderby Mavis,	Bol.	Lindsey,	H. G.
Epworth,	Man.	Lindsey,	C. A.
Evedon,	Asw.	Kesteven,	K. D,
Ewerby,	Asw.	Kesteven,	K. D,
F.			
Faldingworth,	Law.	Lindsey,	F. D.
Farlsthorpe,	Cal.	Lindsey,	G. H.
Farforth,	Lou.	Lindsey,	G. F.
Fenton,	Lov.	Kesteven,	I. B.
Ferriby,	Yar.	Lindsey,	B. C.
Fillingham,	Asla.	Lindsey,	F. C.
Firsby,	Cand.	Lindsey,	H. H.

Names.	Wapontakes.	Grand Division.	Letters.
Fiskerton,	Lawr.	Lindsey,	G. D.
Fishtoft,	Skir.	Holland,	L. G.
Fleet,	Ell.	Holland,	N. G.
Flixburgh,	Man.	Lindsey,	B. B.
FOLKINGHAM,	Ave.	Kesteven,	L. D.
Foston,	Lov.	Kesteven,	K. B.
Foldike,	Kirt.	Holland,	M. F.
Fotherby,	Lud.	Lindsey,	E. F.
Frampton,	Kirt.	Holland,	L. F.
Frieston,	Skir.	Holland,	H. G.
Friskney,	Cand.	Lindsey,	I. H.
Fristhorpe,	Law.	Lindsey,	F. D.
Frodingham,	Man.	Lindsey,	C. B.
Fulbeck,	Lov.	Kesteven,	l. C.
Fulletsby,	Hill.	Lindsey,	G. F.
Fulstow,	Brad.	Lindsey,	E. H.

G.

GAINSBOROUGH,	Man.	Lindsey,	E. A.
Gateburton,	Wal.	Lindsey,	F. B.
Gayton on the Wolds,	Low.	Lindsey,	F. F.
Gayton in the Marsh,	Cal.	Lindsey,	F. G.
Gedney,	Ell.	Holland,	N. G.
Glentworth,	Asla.	Lindsey,	F. C.
Glentham,	Asla.	Lindsey,	E. C.
Goltho,	Wrag.	Lindsey,	G. D.
Gosberton,	Kirt.	Holland,	L. E.
Goulceby,	Gar.	Lindsey,	F. F.
Goutby,	Gar.	Lindsey,	G. E.
Goshill,	Yar.	Lindsey,	B. D.
Grainsby,	Brad.	Lindsey,	D. F.
Grainsthorpe,	Lou.	Lindsey,	G. G.
GRANTHAM,	Gran.	Kesteven,	L. B.
Grasby,	Yar.	Lindsey,	D. D.
Grayingham,	Cor.	Lindsey,	D. B.
Greetham,	Hill.	Lindsey,	G. F.

Gretford

Names.	Wapontakes.	Grand Division.	Letters.
Gretford,	Neſs.	Keſteven,	O. D.
Greetwell,	Lawr.	Lindſey,	G. C.
Grimoldby,	Lou.	Lindſey,	F. G.
GRIMSBY, magna,	Brad.	Lindſey,	C. F.
Grimſby, parva,	Lud.	Lindſey,	E. F.
Gunnerby,	Gran.	Keſteven,	K. B.
Gunby, weſt,	Belt.	Keſteven,	N. B.
Gunby, eaſt,	Cand.	Lindſey,	H. H.
H.			
Haburgh,	Yar.	Lindſey,	B. E.
Hackthorne,	Aſla.	Lindſey,	F. E.
Hacconby,	Ave.	Keſteven,	M. D.
Hagworthingham,	Hill.	Lindſey,	H. G.
Hagnaby,	Bol.	Lindſey,	H. F.
Hainton,	Wrag.	Lindſey,	F. E.
Halton, eaſt,	Yar.	Lindſey,	A. D.
Halton, weſt,	Man.	Lindſey,	A. B.
Hale,	Aſw.	Keſteven,	L. E.
Haltham,	Horn.	Lindſey,	H. F.
Halton holgate,	Bol.	Lindſey,	H. G.
Hallington,	Lou.	Lindſey,	F. F.
Homeringham,	Hill.	Lindſey,	H. F.
Hanworth cold,	Aſh.	Lindſey,	F. C.
Hanworth potter,	Lang.	Keſteven,	H. D.
Hannah,	Cal.	Lindſey,	G. H.
Harmſton,	Boo.	Keſteven,	H. C.
Harlaxton,	Gran.	Keſteven,	L. B.
Harpſwell,	Aſla.	Lindſey,	E. C.
Harrington,	Hill.	Lindſey,	G. F.
Hareby,	Bol.	Lindſey,	H. F.
Hatcliff,	Brad.	Lindſey,	D. E.
Hatton,	Wrag.	Lindſey,	G. E.
Haugnby Aild,	Cal.	Lindſey,	G. G.
Haverby,	Brad.	Lindſey,	D. F.
Haxey,	Man.	Lindſey,	D. A.

Names.	Wapontakes.	Grand Division.	Letters.
Haydor,	Winn.	Kefteven,	L. C.
Heapham,	Cor.	Lindfey,	E. B.
Healing,	Brad.	Lindfey,	C. E.
Heckington,	Afw.	Kefteven,	K. E.
Helpringham,	Afw.	Kefteven,	L. D.
Hemfwell,	Afla.	Lindfey,	C. C.
Heighington,	Lang.	Kefteven,	H. D.
Hemingby,	Gar.	Lindfey,	G. E.
Hibalftow	Man.	Lindfey,	D. C.
Hogfthorpe,	Cal.	Lindfey,	G. H.
Holton Beckering,	Wrag.	Lindfey,	F. D.
Holton le Clay,	Brad.	Lindfey,	D. F.
Holton le Moor,	Wal.	Lindfey,	E. D.
Holliwell,	Bell.	Kefteven,	N. C.
Holbeach,	Ell.	Holland,	N. G.
Horbling,	Ave.	Kefteven,	L. D.
Horkftow,	Yar.	Lindfey,	B. C.
Horfington.	Cor.	Lindfey,	H. I.
HORNCASTLE,	Horn.	Lindfey,	H. F.
Hough,	Lov.	Kefteven,	K. B.
Hougham,	Lov.	Kefteven,	F. F.
Howell,	Afw.	Kefteven,	K. D.
Humberftone,	Brad.	Lindfey,	D. F.
Hundleby,	Bol.	Lindfey,	H. G.
Hunnington,	Winn.	Kefteven,	L. C.
Huttoft,	Cal.	Lindfey,	G. H.
Hykham, nerth,	Boo.	Kefteven,	H. C.
Hykham, fouth,	Boo.	Kefteven,	H. C.
I.			
Immingham,	Yar.	Lindfey,	B. E.
Ingham,	Afla.	Lindfey,	F. C.
Ingoldfby,	Afw.	Kefteven,	L. D.
Ingoldmells,	Cand.	Lindfey,	H. H.
Irby,	Brad.	Lindfey,	C. L.
Irby,	Cand.	Lindfey,	H. H.
Irnham,	Bell.	Kefteven,	M. C.

Kc al

Names.	Wapontakes.	Grand Division.	Letters.
K.			
Keal, eaft,	Bol.	Lindfey,	H. G.
Keal, weft,	Bol.	Lindfey,	H. G.
Keelby by Haydor,	Afw.	Kefteven,	K. C.
Keelby,	Yar.	Lindfey,	C. E.
Kelftorn,	Low.	Lindfey,	E. F.
Kelfey, St. Mary,	Wal.	Lindfey,	D. D.
Kelfey, St. Nicholas,	Wal.	Lindfey,	D. D.
Kelfey, north,	Yar.	Lindfey,	D. D.
Kernington,	Yar.	Lindfey,	C. D.
Kettlethorpe,	Well.	Lindfry,	G. B.
Kiddington,	Lou.	Lindfey,	F. G.
Killingholme,	Yar.	Lindfey,	A. D.
Kingerby,	Wal.	Lindfey,	E. D.
KIRTON, in Lindfey,	Cor.	Lindfey,	D. C.
Kirkby Green,	Lang.	Kefteven,	I. D.
Kirkby on Bain,	Gar.	Lindfey,	H. E.
Kirkby Underwood,	Ave.	Kefteven,	M. D.
Kirkby la Thorpe,	Afw.	Kefteven,	K. D.
Kirkby, weft,	Wal.	Lindfey,	E. D.
Kirkby, eaft,	Bol.	Lindfey,	H. F.
Kirmond,	Wal.	Lindfey,	E. E.
Kirton, in Holland,	Kirt.	Holland,	L. F.
Kirkftead,	Gar.	Lindfey,	I. E.
Knaith,	Well.	Lindfey,	F B.
Kyme,	Afw.	Kefteven,	K. E.
L.			
Laceby,	Brad.	Lindfey,	C. E.
Langton by Wragby,	Wrag.	Lindfey,	G. E.
Langton by Partney,	Hill.	Lindfey,	H. G.
Langton by Horncaftle,	Gar.	Lindfey,	H. E.
Langtoft,	Nefs.	Kefteven,	O. D.
Laffington,	Belt.	Kefteven,	L. C.
Laughton,	Cor.	Lindfey,	D. B.
Lea,	Cor.	Lindfey,	E. B.

Names.	Wapontakes.	Grand Division.	Letters.
Leadenham,	Lov.	Kesteven,	I. C.
Leak,	Skir.	Holland,	K. G.
Legsby,	Wrag.	Lindsey,	F. E.
Legburn,	Lou.	Lindsey,	F. G.
Lessingham,	Flax.	Kesteven,	K. D.
Leverton,	Skir.	Holland,	K. G.
Limber magna,	Yar.	Lindsey,	C. E.
Linwood,	Wal.	Lindsey,	F. D.
Lincoln, St. Buttolph,			
St. Peters of Gouts,			
St. Marks,			
St. Mary,			
St. Benedict,			
St. Swithins,			
St. Martins,			
St. Peters at Arches	Lawr.	Lindsey,	G. C.
St. Michael,			
St. Paul,			
St. Peters, Eastgate,			
St. Margarets,			
St. Nicholas, new,			
St. Mary Magdalen,			
St. John, Newport,			
Lissington,	Wrag.	Lindsey,	F. D.
Londonthorpe,	Gran.	Kesteven,	L. C.
LOUTH,	Lou.	Lindsey,	F. F.
Ludford magna,	Wrag.	Lindsey,	E. E.
Ludford parva,	Wrag.	Lindsey,	E. E.
Ludborough,	Lud.	Lindsey,	E. F.
Luddington,	Man.	Lindsey,	B. B.
Lusby,	Bol.	Lindsey,	H. F.
Lutton,	Ell.	Holland,	M. H.
M.			
Mablethorpe, St. Mary,	Cal.	Lindsey,	F. H.
Mablethorpe, St. Peter,	Cal.	Lindsey,	F. H.

Maltby,

Names.	Wapontakes.	Grand Division.	Letters.
Maltby,	Cal.	Lindfey,	G. G.
Manton,	Man.	Lindfey,	D. C.
Maaby,	Lou.	Lindfey,	F. G.
Marton,	Well.	Lindfey,	F. B.
Martin,	Gar.	Lindfey,	H. E.
Marton,	Lov.	Kefteven,	K. B.
Marth Chapel,	Brad.	Lindfey,	E. H.
Markby,	Cal.	Lindfey,	G H.
Mareham on the Hill,	Horn.	Lindfey,	H. F.
Mareham in the Fen,	Horn.	Lindfey,	H. F.
Melton Rof.	Yar.	Lindfey,	C. D.
Meffingham	Man.	Lindfey,	C. B.
Metheringham,	Lang.	Kefteven,	H. D.
Minagby,	Bol	Lindfey,	H. F.
Minting,	Gar.	Lindfey,	G. E.
Moorby,	Horn	Lindfey,	H. F.
Moorby Branfton,	Lincoln Liberty	Kefteven,	H. C.
Morton,	Ave.	Kefteven,	M. D.
Moulton,	Ell	Holland,	N. F.
Muckton,	Lou.	Lindfey,	G. G.
Mumby,	Cal.	Lindfey,	G. H
N.			
NAVENBY,	Boo.	Kefteven,	H. C.
Nettleham,	Lawr.	Lindfey,	G. C.
Nettleton,	Ya.	Lindfey,	D. E.
Newton by Trent,	Well.	Lindfey,	G. R.
Newton by Sleater,	Ave.	Kefteven,	L. D.
Newton by Toft,	Wel.	Lindfey,	F. D.
Newton L Weld,	Brad.	Lindfey,	D. F.
Nocton,	Lang.	Kefteven,	H. D.
Normanby, eaft,	Afla.	Lindfey,	E. C.
Normanby, weft,	Wel.	Lindfey,	E. D.
Northorpe,	Cor.	Lindfey,	D. B.
North cule,	Boo.	Kefteven,	H. B.
Northholme,	Cand.	Lindfey,	I. K.

Names.	Wapontakes.	Grand Division	Letters.
Norton diſney,	Boo.	Keſteven,	I. B.
Normanton,	Lov.	Keſteven,	K. C.
Norton Biſhop,	Aſla.	Lindſey,	E. C.
O.			
Orby,	Cand.	Lindſey,	H. G.
Ormſby, ſouth,	Hill.	Lindſey,	G. G.
Ormſby, nun,	Lud.	Lindſey,	E. F.
Oſbornby,	Ave.	Keſteven,	L. D.
Oſgodby,	Wal.	Lindſey,	L. D.
Owerſby,	Wal.	Lindſey,	E. D.
Owmby,	Aſla.	Lindſey,	F C.
Ouſton,	Man.	Lindſey,	D. A.
Oxcomb,	Hill.	Lindſey,	G. F.
P.			
Panton,	Wrag.	Lindſey,	G. E.
Partney,	Cand.	Lindſey,	H. G.
Pickworth,	Ave.	Keſteven,	L. D.
Pilham,	Cor.	Lindſey,	E. B.
Pinchbeck,	Ell.	Holland,	M. F.
Ponton magna,	Gran.	Keſteven,	M. C.
Ponton parva,	Winn.	Keſteven,	M. C.
Q.			
Quadring,	Kirt.	Holland,	L. F.
Quarrington,	Aſw.	‚eſteven,	K. D.
R.			
Raithby by Spilſby,	Bol.	Lindſey,	H. G.
Ranby,	Gar.	Lindſey,	G. E.
Rand,	Wrag.	Lindſey,	F. D.
RASIN MARKET,	Wal.	Lindſey,	E. D.
Raſin drax,	Wal.	Lindſey,	E. D.
Raſin Tupholme,	Wal.	Lindſey,	E. D.

Names.	Wapontakes.	Grand Division.	Letters.
Rasin, west,	Wal.	Lindsey,	E. D.
Rathby,	Lou.	Lindsey,	F. F.
Ravendale,	Brad.	Lindsey,	D. E.
Rauceby,	Flax.	Kesteven,	K. C.
Repham,	Lawr.	Lindsey,	G. D.
Reston, south,	Cal.	Lindsey,	F. G.
Reston, north,	Lou.	Lindsey,	F. G.
Retburn,	Man.	Lindsey,	D. E.
Reavesby,	Bol.	Lindsey,	F. F.
Riby,	Yar.	Lindsey,	C. E.
Rigsby,	Cal.	Lindsey,	G. G.
Rippingale,	Ave.	Kesteven,	M. D.
Rischolme,	Lawr.	Lindsey,	G. C.
Ropsley,	Winn.	Kesteven,	L. C.
Rothwell,	Brad.	Lindsey,	D. E.
Roughton,	Horn.	Lindsey,	H. E.
Rowston,	Flax.	Kesteven,	I. D.
Roxby,	Man.	Lindsey,	B. B.
Rutland,	Low.	Lindsey,	G. G.
Ruskington,	Flax.	Kesteven,	I. D.

S.

Names.	Wapontakes.	Grand Division.	Letters.
Sailby,	Cal.	Lindsey,	G. H.
Salmonby,	Hill.	Lindsey,	G. F.
Saltfleetby all Saints,	Lou.	Lindsey,	E. G.
Saltfleetby, St. Clements	Lou.	Lindsey,	F. H.
Saltfleetby, St. Peters	Lou.	Lindsey,	E. H.
Sapperton,	Gran.	Kesteven,	L. C.
Sausthorpe,	Hill.	Lindsey,	H. G.
Saxby,	Yar.	Lindsey,	B. C.
Saxby,	Asla.	Lindsey,	F. C.
Saxilby,	Lawr.	Lindsey,	G. B.
Saleby,	Cal.	Lindsey,	G. H.
Scampton,	Law.	Lindsey,	F. C.

Names.	Wapontakes.	Grand Division.	Letters.
Scawby,	Yan.	Lindfey,	C. C.
Scamblefby,	Gar.	Lindfey,	G. F.
Scotton,	Cor.	Lindfey,	D. B.
Scotter,	Cor.	Lindfey,	D. B.
Scothern,	Lawr.	Lindfey,	G. C.
Scopwick,	Lang.	Kefteven,	I. D.
Scratho,	Brad.	Lindfey,	C. F.
Screvelfby,	Gar.	Lindfey,	H. F.
Scedington,	Afw.	Kefteven,	K. D.
Scremby,	Cand.	Lindfey,	H. G.
Searby,	Yar.	Lindfey,	C. D.
Sedgebrook,	Winn.	Kefteven,	L. B.
Sempringham,	Ave.	Kefteven,	I. C.
Sibley,	Bol.	Lindfey,	K. G.
Sixhills,	Wrag.	Lindfey,	F. E.
Skegnefs,	Cand.	Lindfey,	H. H.
Skellingthorpe,	Boo.	Kefteven,	H. B.
Skinnand,	Boo.	Kefteven,	I. C.
Skirbeck,	Skir.	Holland,	L. H.
Skindleby,	Cand.	Lindfey,	H. G.
Skidbrook,	Lou.	Lindfey,	E. H.
Skillinton,	Bell.	Kefteven,	M. B.
Sleaford,	Flax.	Kefteven,	K. D.
Snarford,	Law.	Lindfey,	F. D.
Snelland,	Wrag.	Lindfey,	F. D.
Snitterby,	Afla.	Lindfey,	E. C.
Sorby,	Wrag.	Lindfey,	G. D.
Somerby,	Yar.	Lindfey,	C. D.
Somerby,	Hill.	Lindfey,	H. F.
Somerby,	Winn.	Kefteven,	L. C.
Somercoats, north,	Lou.	Lindfey,	E. G.
Somercoats, fouth,	Lou.	Lindfey,	E. G.
Southray,	Gar.	Lindfey,	N. F.
Spalding,	Ell.	Holland,	L. D.
Spanby,	Ave.	Kefteven,	H. G.

Spilfby,

Names.	Wapontakes.	Grand Division.	Letters.
SPILSBY,	Bol.	Lindsey,	H. G.
Spriddlington,	Asla.	Lindsey,	F. C.
Springthorpe,	Cor.	Lindsey,	E. B.
Stappleford,	Boo.	Kesteven,	I. B.
Stainton,	Cand.	Kesteven,	H. F.
Stainton, west,	Wrag.	Lindsey,	G. D.
Stainton le hole,	Wal.	Lindsey,	E. E.
Stainton Market,	Gar.	Lindsey,	F. E.
Stainfield,	Wrag.	Lindsey,	G. D.
Stanigot,	Gar.	Lindsey,	F. F.
STAMFORD, St. Mary, St. Michael, St. John, St. George, All Saints,	Ness.	Kesteven,	O. D.
Stallingborough,	Yar.	Lindsey,	C. E.
Steanby,	Belt.	Kesteven,	M. B.
Steeping magna,	Cand.	Lindsey,	H. G.
Steeping parva,	Bol.	Lindsey,	H. G.
Stewton,	Low.	Lindsey,	F. G.
Strixwold,	Gar.	Lindsey,	H. E.
Stixford,	Bol.	Lindsey,	I. F.
Stickney,	Bol.	Lindsey,	I. F.
Stow magna,	Wal.	Lindsey,	F. B.
Stow parva,	Ness.	Kesteven,	O. D.
Stoke, north,	Winn.	Kesteven,	M. B.
Stoke, south,	Gran.	Kesteven,	M. B.
Stragglethorpe,	Lov.	Kesteven,	I B.
Stroxton,	Winn.	Kesteven,	M. B.
Stubby,	Cal.	Lindsey,	G. G.
Stubton,	Lov.	Kesteven,	I. B.
Sudbrook,	Lawr.	Lindsey,	G. C.
Surfleet,	Kirt.	Holland,	M. F.
Sutterton,	Kirt.	Holland,	L. F.
Sutterby,	Cand.	Lindsey,	G. G.

Sutton

Names.	Wapontakes.	Grand Division.	Letters.
Sutton long,	Ell.	Holland,	N. H.
Sutton by Sea,	Cal.	Lindsey,	G. H.
Swafield,	Bell.	Kesteven,	M. C.
Swayton,	Ave.	Kesteven,	L. E.
Swarby,	Asw.	Kesteven,	L. D.
Swaby,	Cal.	Lindsey,	G. G.
Swallow,	Brad.	Lindsey,	D. E.
Swinestead,	Bell.	Kesteven,	M. C.
Swinderby,	Boo.	Kesteven,	H. B.
Swineshead,	Kirt.	Holland,	L. E.
Swinop,	Wal.	Lindsey,	E. E.
Syston,	Winn.	Kesteven,	L. C.

T.

Names.	Wapontakes.	Grand Division.	Letters.
Tallington,	Ness.	Kesteven,	O. D.
Tattershall,	Gar.	Lindsey,	I. E.
Tathwell,	Lou.	Lindsey,	F. F.
Tealby,	Wal.	Lindsey,	E. E.
Tetford,	Hill.	Lindsey,	G. F.
Tetney,	Brad.	Lindsey,	D. G.
Tidd, St. Mary,	Ell.	Holland,	N. H.
Timberland,	Lang.	Kesteven,	I. D.
Theddlethorpe, all Staints,	Cal.	Lindsey,	F. H.
Theddlethorpe, St. Helens	Cal.	Lindsey,	F. H.
Thimbleby,	Horn.	Lindsey,	H. E.
Thornton,	Gai.	Lindsey,	H. E.
Thornton le Moor,	Well.	Lindsey,	D. D.
Thornton Curtis,	Yar.	Lindsey,	B. D.
Thorpe on the Hill,	Boo.	Kesteven,	H. B.
Thorpe, east,	Cand.	Lindsey,	I. H.
Thoresby, north,	Brad.	Lindsey,	D. F.
Thoresby, south,	Cal.	Lindsey,	G. G.
Thoresway,	Wal.	Lindsey,	D. E.
Threckingham,	Ave.	Kesteven,	L. D.
Thurlby,	Boo.	Kesteven,	H. B.

Thurgunby,

Names.	Wapontakes.	Grand Division.	Letters.
Thurgunby,	Wal.	Lindfey,	D. E.
Thurlly le Fen,	Nefs.	Kefteven,	N. D.
Toft,	Well.	Lindfey,	E. C.
Toniton fuperior,	Horn.	Lindfey.	H. F.
Toniton inferior,	Horn.	Lindfey,	H. F.
Toniton, St. Peters,	ol.	Lindfe ,	H. G.
Toniton, all Saints,	Fol.	Lindfey,	J. G.
Torkfey,	Well.	Lindfey,	F. E.
Torrington, eaft,	Wrag.	Lindfey,	F. E.
Torrington, weft,	Wrag.	Lindfey,	F. E.
Tothill,	Cal.	Lindfey,	G. G.
Trufthorpe,	Cal.	Lindfey,	F. H.
U.			
Uffington,	Nefs.	Kefteven,	O. D.
Ulceby,	Yar.	Lindfey,	B. D.
Ulceby,	Cal.	Lindfey,	G. G.
Upton,	Well.	Lindfey,	F. B.
Uttelby,	Well.	Lindfey,	E. D.
Utterby,	Lud.	Lindfey,	E. F.
W.			
Waddingham,	Cor.	Lindfey,	D. C.
Waddington,	Lincoln Liberty	Kefteven,	H. C.
Waddingworth,	Gar.	Lindfey,	G. E.
WAINFLEET, all Saints,	Cand.	Lindfey,	I. H.
Wainfleet, St. Mary,	Cand.	Lindfey,	I. H.
Waith,	Brad.	Lindfey,	D. F.
Walcot,	Avc.	Kefteven,	L. D.
Walefby,	Wal.	Lindfey,	E. D.
Waltham,	Brad.	Lindfey,	D. F.
Walmfingburgh,	Lang.	Kefteven,	C. H.
Welbourn,	boo.	Kefteven	I. C.
Welby,	Winn.	Kefteven,	C. K.
Welton,	Lou.	Lindfey,	F. F.

Names.	Wapontakes.	Grand Division.	Letters.
Welton,	Lawr.	Lindsey,	F. C.
Welton, in the Marsh,	Cand.	Lindsey,	H. H.
Well,	Cal.	Lindsey,	G. G.
Weston,	Ell.	Holland,	M. F.
Westborough,	Lov.	Kesteven,	K. B.
Whaplode,	Ell.	Holland,	N. G.
Whitton,	Man.	Lindsey,	A B.
Wickenby,	Wrag.	Lindsey,	F. D.
Wickam Chapel,	Ell	Holland,	M. F.
Wigtoft,	Kirt.	Holland,	L. F.
Willingham by Stow,	Well.	Lindsey,	F. B.
Willingore,	Boo.	Kesteven,	I. C.
Willingham Cherry,	Lawr.	Lindsey,	G. C.
Willsthorpe,	Ness.	Kesteven,	N. D.
Willingham north,	Wal.	Lindsey,	E. E.
Willingham, south,	Wrag.	Lindsey,	F. E.
Willoughton,	Asla.	Lindsey,	E. B.
Willsford,	Winn.	Kesteven,	K. C.
Wilksby,	Horn.	Lindsey,	H. F.
Willoughby le sen.	Cal.	Lindsey,	G. H.
Willoughby Silk,	Asw.	Kesteven,	K. D.
Willoughby Scot,	Ave.	Kesteven,	L. D.
Winterton,	Man.	Lindsey,	B. B.
Winteringham,	Man.	Lindsey,	A. B.
Winceby,	Hill.	Lindsey,	H. F.
Winthorpe,	Cand.	Lindsey,	H. H.
Wispington,	Gar.	Lindsey,	G. E.
Witham on the Hill,	Bell.	Kesteven,	N. D.
Witham, north,	Bell.	Kesteven,	N. C.
Witham, south,	Belt.	Kesteven,	N. C.
Withcall,	Lou.	Lindsey,	F. F.
Withern,	Cal.	Lindsey,	G. G.
Woolsthorpe,	Winn.	Kesteven,	L. B.
Worlaby,	Yar.	Lindsey,	C. C.
Wotton,	Yar.	Lindsey,	B. D.

Names.	Wapontakes.	Grand Divifion.	Letters.
WRAGBY,	Wrag.	Lindfey,	G D.
Wrangle,	Skir.	Holland,	K. G.
Wrawby,	Yar.	Lindfey,	C. C.
Wroote,	Man.	Lindfey,	D. A.
Wyberton,	Kirt.	Holland,	L. F.
Wyham,	Lud.	Lindfey,	E. F.
Y.			
Yarborough,	Lou.	Lindfey,	E. G.

Tho' it appears by the above Lift, that the Number of Parifhes in the County is 630, yet I do not believe that is the real Number. I have had Lifts from both the Ecclefiaftical and Civil Officers, as from the Regifter's Office, and alfo from the Commiffioners of Land-Tax, and Clerks of the Peace, none of which agree. The Reafon I have found; that it not being agreed upon, what may properly be called a Parifh, there being feveral Places called Parifhes in the Regifter's Lift, that are not Places of Worfhip; as MEER, near LINCOLN; KIRKSTEAD, near HORNCASTLE; RISEHOLM, near LINCOLN, &c. On the other Hand the Commiffioners Lifts reckon feveral Places, Parifhes, as they are feperate Collections; maintain their own Poor, have a Conftable and Parifh Officers; as CLEETHAM, near KIRTON; FENTON, near KETTLETHORPE; and many others.

Distances on the Roads in *Lincolnshire,*

MEASURED from *Lincoln Minster* to the Boundary of the County, with the Distance from that Boundary to *London,* and the total from *Lincoln* to *London.*

N. B. The Miles are numbered as paid for.

From Lincoln to Stamford, the Post-Road.	Miles.	
Green Man, *on the Heath,*		8
Ancaster,	12	20
Grantham,	7	27
Coltsterworth,	8	35
Witham Common,	2	37
Stamford, *the Boundary,*	11	48
London,	89	137

To Stamford, *another way.*		
Ancaster *as above,*		20
Cold-Harbour,	5	25
Coltsterworth,	8	33
Stamford,	13	45
London,	89	135

To Market Deeping, *Coach and Fly Road.*		
Green Man, *as above,*		8
Sleaford,	10	18
Folkingham,	9	27
Bourn,	9	36
J. Deeping, *the Boundary,*	8	44
London,	89	133

From Lincoln to J. Deeping	Miles.	
Sleaford, *as before,*		18
Swineshead,	11	29
Gosberton,	4	33
Spalding,	6	39
J. Deeping, *the Boundary,*	12	51
London,	89	140

From Lincoln to Long Sutton, *and the Boundary.*		
Spalding, *as above,*		39
Holbech,	8	47
Long Sutton,	5	52
Tid-Gout, *the Boundary,*	4	56
London,	95	151

From Lincoln to Boston, by Horncastle, and the boundary *as before.*		
Langworth Bridge,		6
Wragby,	5	11
Horncastle,	10	21
Leak-Gates,	8	29
Boston,	12	41
Fofdyke-Wash,	9	50
Saracen's-Head,	3	53
Wash-Way to Fleet-Bull,	5	58
Tid-Gout, *the Boundary,*	6	64
London,	95	159

Another way to Boston,		Miles.	CROSS ROADS.		Miles.
Sleaford as before,		18			
Heckington,	5	23	From Lincoln to Grimsby, Post-Road.		
Swineshead,	6	29			
Boston,	6	35	Wragby as before,		11
			Hainton,		17
From Lincoln to Crowland, and the Boundary there.			Market Raisin,	6	23
			Binbrook,	9	32
Spalding as before,		39	Brigfly,	6	38
Crowland, Post-Road,	10	49	Grimsby,	5	43
Boundary south of that	2	51	From Lincoln to Louth and Saltfleet.		
London,	92	143			
From Lincoln to the Boundary at Cross-keys Wash.			Wragby as before,		11
			Hainton, and to Tibb's Inn,	8	19
Fleet Bell as before,		58	Louth,	9	28
Long Sutton,	4	62	Saltfleet,	10	38
Cross-Keys Wash,	6	68	From Lincoln to Gainsborough.		
Lynn-Regis,	7	75			
From Lincoln, northwards.			Saxilby Bridge,		6
Spittle on the Street,		12	Torksey,	5	11
Glanford Briggs,	12	24	Gainsborough,	7	18
Barton Waterside,	12	36	From Lincoln to Newark.		
Cross the Humber to Hull,	7	43			
Another Road into Yorkshire.			Potters Hill, the Bound,		13
To near Redborn,		16	Newark,	5	18
Appleby,	17	28	From Lincoln to Spilsby, &c		
Winteringham,	5	33	Horncastle as before,		21
Cross the Humber to Burgh,	3	36	Spilsby,	10	31
			Burgh,	7	38
			Wainfleet,	4	42

From Lincoln to Grantham on the *Cliff-row*.		Miles.
Waddington,		5
Leadenham,	9	14
Hunnington,	7	21
Belton,	4	25
Grantham,	2	27

Great Drove-Road or Watling-Street, from Barton, *southwards*.		
To *near* Melton-Rofs,		8
Caiftoithong,	10	18
Tibb's Inn,	12	30
Horncaftle,	10	40
Leadigate,	8	48
Bofton,	12	60

Turnpike Road from Gainsborough to Louth.		
Harpfwell,		7
Bifhop Brigg,	7	14
Market Railin,	5	19
Ludford,	6	25
Louth,	8	33

Drove Road from Littleborough to Horncaftle.		
Tilbriggs,		6
Langworth,	10	16
Wragby,	5	21
Horncaftle,	10	31

From Newark to Sleaford, *Crofs the Heath*.		Miles.
Beckingham,		5
Leadenham,	6	11
Bayard's-leap *on High-ftreet*,	4	15
Sleaford,	6	21

From Brigg to Caiftor and Louth.		
Somerby,		5
Caiftor,	5	10
Binbroke,	7	17
Louth,	10	27

From Brigg to Grimfby.		
Melton-Rofs,		6
Great Limber,	5	11
Grimfby,	8	19

From Stamford to Newark, and Gainfborough.		
Grantham,		21
Newark,	14	35
Torkfey,	18	53
Gainfborough,	7	60

From Bourn to Coltfterworth.		
Grimthorpe,		5
Corby,	3	8
Coltfterworth,	4	12

From Stamford to Bourn.		
Toft,		7
Bourn,	6	13

TABLE of TIDES and FERRY-BOATS paffing from BARTON to HULL, and return.

Moon's Age.		High Water.		Coming in.		Going out.	
Days.		H.	M.	H.	M	H.	M.
1	16	7	3	5	10	7	40
2	17	7	51	5	58	8	30
3	18	8	39	7	20	9	20
4	19	9	27	8	10	10	12
5	20	10	16	9	4	10	40
6	21	11	5	9	50	11	30
7	22	11	54	10	40	12	15
8	23	12	45	11	20	1	14
9	24	I	29	12	20	2	0
10	25	2	17	1	4	2	55
11	26	3	4	2	10	3	50
12	27	3	52	2	45	4	30
13	28	4	40	3	30	5	10
14	29	5	27	4	18	6	0
15	30	6	15	5	0	7	10

It is the Bufinefs of a Paffenger to attend at the Time fhewn by this Table; tho' on account of High Winds, frefh Floods, &c the coming in, or going out, may vary; but *Patience* is recommended.

A TABLE for paſſing over CROSS-KEYS and FOSS-DIKE-WASHES, in the County of LINCOLN.

Moon's Age.		Full Sea.		Begin to paſs over				End paſſing over.			
				Foſs dike Waſh.		Croſs keys Waſh.		Foſs dike Waſh.		Croſs keys Waſh.	
Days		H.	M.	H.	M.	H.	M.	H.	M.	H.	M.
1	16	7	0	10	0	10	30	4	15	3	35
2	17	7	48	10	48	11	18	5	33	4	23
3	18	8	36	11	36	12	6	6	21	5	11
4	19	9	24	12	24	12	54	7	9	5	59
5	20	10	12	1	12	1	42	7	57	6	47
6	21	11	0	2	0	2	30	8	45	7	35
7	22	11	48	2	48	3	18	9	33	8	23
8	23	12	36	3	36	4	6	10	21	9	11
9	24	1	24	4	24	4	54	11	9	9	59
10	25	2	12	5	12	5	42	11	57	10	47
11	26	3	0	6	0	6	30	12	45	11	35
12	27	3	48	6	48	7	18	1	33	12	23
13	28	4	36	7	36	8	6	2	21	1	11
14	29	5	24	8	24	8	54	3	9	1	59
15	30	6	12	9	12	9	42	3	57	2	47

Tho' this Table ſhews the Time of paſſing the Waſhes yet extraordinary High Winds, or great freſh Floods, will cauſe a difference of Time, but as there are always Guides to attend, *hey* are the beſt Judges.

F I N I S.

CPSIA information can be obtained at www.ICGtesting.com
Printed in the USA
LVOW11s1924190114

370040LV00009B/331/P